NAVIGATING
with or without
A COMPASS

Using Bearings and Nature
to Find Your Way

MILES TANNER

BLACK DOG
& LEVENTHAL
PUBLISHERS
NEW YORK

Black Dog & Leventhal Publishers
Hachette Book Group
1290 Avenue of the Americas
New York, NY 10104

www.hachettebookgroup.com
www.blackdogandleventhal.com

First Edition: May 2019

Black Dog & Leventhal Publishers is an imprint of Running Press, a division of Hachette Book Group. The Black Dog & Leventhal Publishers name and logo are trademarks of Hachette Book Group, Inc.

The publisher is not responsible for websites (or their content) that are not owned by the publisher.

The Hachette Speakers Bureau provides a wide range of authors for speaking events. To find out more, go to www.HachetteSpeakersBureau.com or call (866) 376-6591.

Print book interior design by Paul Barrett
Produced by Girl Friday Productions

Image credits: 14, Golden Koi 88/Shutterstock; 16, Daria Chupinina/Shutterstock; 17, Andrii-Oliinyk/Getty Images; 19, Nastasic/Getty Images; 22, Makhnach_M/Getty Images; 23, Maxger/Shutterstock; 26, tmietty/Getty Images; 32 (rope & knife) ivan-96/Getty Images, (matchbox) channarongsds/Getty Images; 35, DenPotisev/Getty Images; 44, Vectorpocket/Shutterstock; 46, Pimpay/Getty Images; 47, Vectorgoods studio/Shutterstock; 48, Pimpay/Getty Images; 49, Harry Bates; 50, Iryna Kashpur/Shutterstock; 52, Pimpay/Getty Images; 54, tutsi/Shutterstock; 60, Harry Bates; 61, suricoma/Getty Images; 62, Harry Bates; 63, Harry Bates; 64, Pimpay/Getty Images; 65, Pimpay/Getty Images; 67, Harry Bates; 75, Pimpay/Getty Images; 76, Morphart Creation/Shutterstock; 78, bauhaus1000/Getty Images; 83, Vecteezy.com; 84, Brandon Laufenberg/Getty Images; 87, USGS; 89, VectorGoods/Getty Images; 94, Grigoriy Kozlovskikh/Shutterstock; 96, Harry Bates; 98, Harry Bates; 99, (map) Bardocz Peter/Shutterstock, (declination) Harry Bates; 101, channarongsds/Getty Images; 103, andrey oleynik/Shutterstock; 106, Pimpay/Getty Images; 108, Pimpay/Getty Images; 112, ambassador806/Getty Images; 116, Maiia Vysotska/Shutterstock

LCCN: 2018961628
ISBNs: 978-0-7624-9396-8 (paper over board), 978-0-7624-9399-9 (ebook)

Printed in China

1010

10 9 8 7 6 5 4 3 2 1

Dedicated to all those who
seek direction from the North Star

Contents

Introduction 11

CHAPTER 1: History of Navigation 14

CHAPTER 2: How to Avoid Getting Lost 26

CHAPTER 3: Natural Observations 44

CHAPTER 4: The Sun, Moon, and Stars 52

CHAPTER 5: The Map 78

CHAPTER 6: The Compass 94

CHAPTER 7: Beyond a Map and Compass 112

CHAPTER 8: Exercises 116

Final Advice 123

Navigation Notes 125

We are born to wander through a chaos field. And yet we do not become hopelessly lost, because each walker who comes before us leaves behind a trace for us to follow.

ROBERT MOOR, *ON TRAILS*

Introduction

Navigational know-how is sometimes overlooked as a rudimentary skill that you can intuitively learn without much study—just observe your surroundings and walk from point A to point B. But when you dig past the surface of the science of navigation, you'll find that a whole world of technical (and practical) knowledge awaits.

Some people assume that navigation is a skill set studied only by survivalists. But any person who ventures into the outdoors—or who simply wants to find their way around a city without a smartphone—should learn at a minimum the basics of route-finding, compass-reading, and map-reading. Not only can it be a fun hobby to learn, but it may also save your life.

As you dive in to this book, you'll learn that navigation has played a central role in the advancement of civilization and exploration for thousands of years. At the very least, examples of ancient problem-solving and invention will remind you how resourceful humans can be when motivated by necessity. Early civilizations looked to the sky for guidance on how to navigate. The first mapmakers used clay, shells, and wood to render replicas of their surroundings. Bygone sailors may have even observed the flight patterns of birds or noted certain smells wafting from shore in order to gauge their bearings at sea.

These days, technology has advanced enough that devices can essentially do the work of navigation for us. But devices can run out of battery or lose a charge. Unpredictable changes in weather can obscure landmarks. Strong currents can push watercraft off course. These common scenarios often result in veering off route. To correct the situation and stay safe, more sophisticated navigation skills are needed.

Before participating in activities where getting lost could have dangerous repercussions, it's a good idea to learn the basics of navigating using simple—and essential—tools like a compass and a map. Even the most experienced outdoorspeople get lost, and it is often because they left these tools behind. That's why this book will cover not only the basics, but also more technical navigation techniques like calculating bearings, noting the positions of celestial bodies, and creating your own solar compass.

Even non-outdoorsy people can benefit from learning the art of navigation. Some people may rarely think about north versus south, the divisions of time, or how to use a printed map to plan a route, because we let our technological tools do this work for us. As an unintended consequence, we've grown increasingly unaware and ignorant of our surroundings. Not only is there a practicality in knowing how to find your way, but there is beauty in the art of reading the signs that nature provides. In a sense, learning how to navigate is like

❝ Not only is there a practicality in knowing how to find your way, but there is beauty in the art of reading the signs that nature provides. ❞

learning a new language. Knowing how to read nature's language allows us to understand new information about our surroundings, helping us to not only avoid getting lost, but also deepen our appreciation for all that the natural world has to teach us. Learning how to find north from the location of the stars, determine east from the position of the sun, and use your natural awareness to guide you may awaken an excitement that comes from understanding the natural world.

This book is an excellent first step toward developing those skills, which will lead to a clearer sense of direction—in the city or the woods.

1

History of Navigation

—— ✕ ——

Mapping the Early World

> *"Not until we are lost do we begin
> to understand ourselves."*
>
> Henry David Thoreau

Navigation is the means by which a person can pinpoint their geographic location and then accurately determine where they need to travel to reach their intended destination. Although this can seem simple, there's an art to the science.

The first sailors followed the coastline, keeping land in sight, as this was the safest way to avoid getting lost at sea. The Greeks may have also used clouds and smell as navigational clues, since weather tends to form over landmasses, and odors can drift far across the ocean. Polynesians would watch the pattern and color of the waves, which when observed with expert eyes can indicate the direction of land. Sailors in ancient cultures also used the reliable nature of trade winds and currents to push them in the right direction.

On land, physical features are good points of reference for determining distance and position. Natural landmarks like mountains, rivers, and lakes can be used as geographic coordinates. But when civilizations began to cross long distances over deserts and oceans, a more precise method for calculating fixed positions became necessary.

Eventually, a grid system was developed, which marked latitudinal and longitudinal lines across a global map.

Latitude measures the distance from the equator, delineated by east-west lines that run parallel to the equator on a map of the world. These latitudinal lines are called "parallels" and are measured in

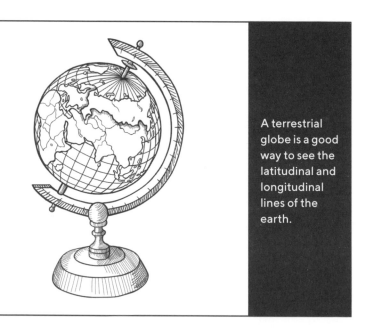

A terrestrial globe is a good way to see the latitudinal and longitudinal lines of the earth.

degrees. For example, the value of the parallel at the equator is zero degrees latitude, with the North Pole measuring 90 degrees north, and the South Pole measuring 90 degrees south.

Longitudinal lines are like latitudinal lines, except that they extend north to south, running parallel to the prime meridian, which divides the world into the Western and Eastern Hemispheres. Longitudinal lines are called "meridians" and, like latitudinal lines, the distance between each line is called a degree. On average, one degree of longitude or latitude measures approximately sixty-nine miles. There are 360 degrees of longitude around the globe and 180 degrees of latitude. Each degree, of either longitude or latitude, can be divided into 60-minute units, which can further be divided

AS THE CROW FLIES

At high latitudes, where the summer sky obscures the stars, different means of navigation have become necessary. The Vikings would note the flight patterns of birds. An early Norwegian explorer known by the nickname Raven-Floki sailed with ravens on his expedition to Iceland. He starved the ravens until he needed to locate the nearest landmass, at which point, he released the hungry birds in hopes that they would fly toward land in search of food. One flew away and then returned. The second flew over the boat and came back as well. The third left and did not return, and so Ravin-Floki set off in the direction of the third raven's flight path. Eventually, he reached shore.

into 60 seconds. These units, however, don't correspond to measurements of time.

The lines of longitude and latitude form a grid pattern. The point where a parallel and a meridian intersect is called a coordinate, which can be used to determine an exact location on Earth. For example, the latitude coordinate for New York is written as 40°42' N, which translates to 40 degrees and 42 minutes north of the equator. The longitude coordinate is 74°00' W, which means it's 74 degrees and zero minutes west of the prime meridian.

METHODS OF NAVIGATION

Humans have been developing navigational tools for thousands of years. Ancient civilizations used a variety of navigational systems to guide their way, some of which are still being used to this day.

DEAD RECKONING

While the term may seem ominous, dead reckoning is simply a method of wayfinding that doesn't depend on a clear sky and being able to see the stars. Rather, it involves determining a geographic position by noting a previous location, called a "fix," and then using the velocity and direction traveled to estimate the current location. Dead reckoning is also used in nautical and aerial navigation, but lacks precision given uncontrollable variables like current and wind, which can shift the location of any point, making it difficult to find a fix. Since watercraft and aircraft are constantly in motion, this increases the challenge of calculating any given location with accuracy.

SUN AND STARS

One of the most common navigational methods humans have used, celestial navigation, involves using the positions of the sun, stars, and moon to find north and south. The most basic navigational method was simply to use the position of the sun to find east and west. The Phoenicians named east and west *Asu* (sunrise) and *Ereb* (sunset), the eponymous roots for the eastern and western continents Asia and Europe. Celestial navigation also requires a familiarity with the constellations, the positions of which are dependent on the time of year and whether you happen to be looking up at the night sky in the Northern or Southern Hemisphere.

For more accurate measurements, ancient cultures would employ sophisticated instruments to help determine latitude, like the Arabian *kamal*, the astrolabe used by sailors in the Middle Ages, or the gnomon used in China. A sextant is another useful tool in celestial navigation, in that it measures with precision the angle between objects in the sky and the horizon, which helps to determine a location with accuracy. A clock and an almanac are also necessary for the celestial navigator, used in tandem to establish the location of the constellations during a specific time of year and time of night.

COMPASS

The ancient Chinese may have been the earliest civilization to use the compass—an instrument with a needle that points toward magnetic north, which is affected by the earth's magnetic field. Because the earth's magnetic poles aren't fixed on its axis, magnetic north will vary depending on your location. True north is earth's true geographic

An astrolabe estimates and predicts the position of the moon, stars, and planets.

north. To give an accurate reading, most modern compasses will account for the magnetic declination between the two norths.

If there is one instrument that is essential to navigation, it is the trusty compass—equally accurate at sea or on a mountaintop, in snow or summer heat. The first compasses were made of a magnetized needle fixed to a piece of cork or wood that would float freely in a pan of water. Like the process of dead reckoning, compasses were possibly used as backup tools when the sun and stars were not visible. But the accuracy of compass technology quickly helped it become one of the most widely used navigational tools, and one that is still used by many ships and airplanes today.

PILOTING

Piloting, a technique involving the use of fixed points or physical landmarks to get a read on one's geographic location, is used more on land than at sea.

RADIO NAVIGATION

This form of navigation uses radio frequencies to pinpoint an exact geographic location. Radar technology is a type of radio navigation.

GPS

Global Positioning System (GPS) technology works in a similar way to radio navigation, except that instead of focusing only on radio frequencies, GPS hones in on satellites to find the exact geographic coordinates of an object on Earth. GPS devices can also be used to plot routes, look up rough maps of an area, and send a signal with your exact location to emergency rescue services.

CARDINAL DIRECTIONS

Cardinal directions refer to the four points in the compass rose: north, south, east, and west. These are the most common directions referred to in navigation.

A BRIEF HISTORY OF CARTOGRAPHY

Maps have taken a variety of forms throughout human history. In the 1800s, it was discovered that in the Arctic, Inuit fishermen would carve coastal landmarks onto driftwood. Around 700 to 500 BC in Mesopotamia, a map of the world was made from a clay tablet that

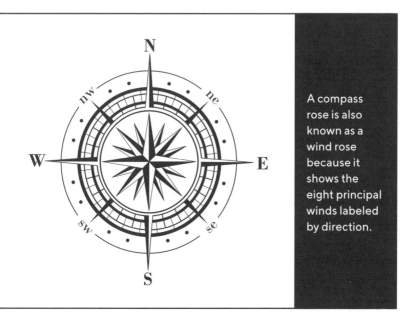

A compass rose is also known as a wind rose because it shows the eight principal winds labeled by direction.

placed Babylon at the center, with the Euphrates River running through the middle, and ocean surrounding the landmass on all sides.

Ancient Greeks have been credited with founding more accurate cartography, which used scientific reasoning to determine scale, in addition to longitude and latitude. The Greek scholar Claudius Ptolemy was the first to use geometry to produce a rectangular-shaped map of the world using the latitude-longitude grid system. Although his map was a Mediterranean-centric drawing that didn't include the Americas, much of Africa or the East, or the Pacific and Atlantic Oceans, his map was the most accurate approximation of the global layout at that time.

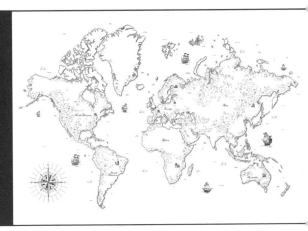

It wasn't until the late eighteenth century that a full picture of the earth and all its features took form visually.

In 1402, a Korean team of royal astronomers created a map that predominantly displays Asia, with Europe and Africa taking up a small portion of the image. Kwon Kun, a neo-Confucian scholar, led the project. The most notable—and historically significant—aspect of the map is that north is at the top. This could be explained by the fact that it's customary to look north in respect to the emperor in Asian imperial ideology. Regardless of the reasoning behind the orientation, this was one of the first maps to use north as a reference point.

❝ A world map created in 1507 by German Martin Waldseemüller would become one of the most valuable in cartographic history. ❞

ARE MODERN MAPS INFALLIBLE?

Even as maps have gotten increasingly realistic, it's worth remembering that no map is a completely accurate representation of the topography. For one, some features are just too small to make it onto the map. Even maps that use photography and satellite imagery as their base are affected by the atmosphere and how that influences aerial photography and satellite captures. Lastly, there is also the human component. Even with computer advances and geographic information systems (GIS), because maps are produced by humans they can still be influenced by bias or error. That said, maps are still incredibly useful for navigation. One could even say, we'd be lost without them!

A world map created in 1507 by German Martin Waldseemüller would become one of the most valuable in cartographic history, after it was sold by a German prince to the Library of Congress for $10 million in 2003. Since it was the first map of the world to render an image of the Americas as a separate landmass from the rest of the globe, it became essentially the birth certificate of America, thus inflating the map's value.

In 1569, along came a map that would become as influential in the advancement of cartography as Ptolemy's map that included longitude and latitude. Gerardus Mercator, a Flemish-German mapmaker, created a map for European navigators that tried to capture the curvature of the earth on a flat surface.

By 1744, the first map with a detailed geographic accounting of a nation-state was making its debut, marking a change in the level of detail applied to maps of smaller regions. Its increased scale allowed for more accurate depictions of geography as well. Four generations of Louis the XIV's family in France oversaw the creation of a map that would catalog the entire nation using triangulation, which uses the measurement of a series of triangles to determine the distances and positions of geographic points.

With advancements in the accuracy and mass reproduction of maps, explorers began traveling farther afield, adding new geographic details with each new voyage. By the late eighteenth century, enough of the world had been mapped that a full picture of the earth and all its features began to take form. Modern cartography now uses computer technology and satellites to create incredibly detailed and accurate maps of anywhere in the world.

2

How to Avoid Getting Lost

— ✕ —

Stop, Think, Observe, and Plan

*"I would rather die walking than die of
boredom reading about how to walk safely."*

Tristan Gooley

During the summers in high school, I stayed on my grandfather's farm in eastern Ohio. It was fifty-one acres with an
old farmhouse and a huge old barn. There was an orchard
in the front, a small Indian mound, and a huge field where crops
were planted. And in the back, along the west side, there was a dense
forest with a small stream flowing through it.

When I arrived for my first summer, my uncle took me out back,
through the field and through the woods, past a dirt road that defined
the western border of the farm, and out to a lake that a neighbor had
made. The neighbor was a lawyer who lived in Cleveland, and only
came out here occasionally. My uncle said it was OK to go to the lake
during the hot days of summer and swim.

A few days later when my uncle was away at work, I decided to go
and check out the lake again and study some of the plants of the area.
I headed out through the large field and entered the woods where I
remembered going with my uncle. There was no discernible trail, so I
just tried to follow where my uncle had walked. The woods were full

of branches and brambles, and I was forced to walk this way and that. The tree canopy was so dense that I couldn't even see rays of sunlight filtering toward the forest floor.

So I just kept walking toward the lake, avoiding the thorns of the berry vines, moving out of the way of the poison oak, and stopping here and there to look at unusual plants. Eventually, I came to a clearing, but the dirt road wasn't there. Instead, the forest opened to a grassy field. I assumed that I'd wandered a bit to the south, so I continued walking, figuring I'd come to the road that would lead me to the lake. I was already tired and soaked with sweat from the heat of the day and the humidity of the forest.

I walked over a slight hill and wondered why I still didn't see the dirt road. Before long, there was a farmhouse. As I approached, I noticed the large barn off to the left. Suddenly, I stopped and looked around, dumbstruck. That was our farmhouse! How was it possible that I was 180 degrees off course? At that moment, I realized how easy it was to get lost.

Determined to get to the lake, I walked back to the woods and entered the slight opening that my uncle had shown me. This time, I didn't just casually walk through the woods. I deliberately picked out two trees that were in-line with each other so I could walk in a straight path as much as was possible through the thick woods. I lined up two more trees and made a beeline again straight toward the far end of the woods where I believed the lake to be. This time, I paid attention to the barely noticeable trail through the woods that others had taken. There was the semblance of a path, though it was not obvious. To keep on course, I continued to deliberately line up trees. Before long, I found the road, and just down the road a bit, there was the lake!

> **"** Anyone who has gotten lost before will understand the urge to never to lose their way again, especially when the consequences of staying lost are dire. **"**

I went swimming, and then easily found my way back through the woods to the farmhouse. I spent the summer studying each turn of the trail and every tree in the forest until I knew the terrain by heart. From that summer on, I never got lost again.

The feeling of being lost is truly uncomfortable. Anyone who has gotten lost before will understand the urge to never to lose their way again, especially when the consequences of staying lost are dire. Luckily, studies show that humans do have an innate sense of direction. But it's somewhat of a "use it or lose it" skill. You have to hone your navigation skills—and strengthen that part of your brain—with practice, experience, and efforts to familiarize yourself with any new territory.

I didn't have a map or a compass when I got lost on my grandfather's farm. But that didn't stop me from finding my way. Having the right provisions, the right mind-set, and some knowledge of nature may be enough to get you from lost to found.

WHY DO PEOPLE GET LOST?

There are countless reasons why people get lost, though some are more common than others.

After a lost person is found, they often say that they simply went out for what they thought would be a short walk. Then, when unexpected weather occured, they did not have the basic supplies that could have prevented them from becoming disoriented, because they didn't expect to be out long.

And, if you're just out for a casual stroll, you go where it is familiar, comfortable, and where you feel there is no danger of getting lost or mixed up. In familiar terrain, you don't make the same effort to observe your surroundings as you would if you thought your life depended on it.

Sometimes, the lost hiker will have ventured into an area that they'd only seen on social media, which seldom shows any of the dangers. It may portray a long and strenuous journey as deceptively low-key and doable.

Another reason people get lost is that they are having such a good time that they ignore their surroundings. Maybe they are deep in conversation with a travel partner, or they're marveling at the flowers and insects and vistas. They might come to a split in the trail and not make a mental note of which direction to go on the return trip. They forget to look back to identify prominent landmarks or changes in topography. Then, when they finally decide to head back to their car, it turns out they've gone a bit farther than expected, and now the trail looks different. They have no idea where they are, or how to find their way back.

A person's ability to navigate can be greatly impaired by drugs or alcohol. It should go without saying that activities like driving, hiking, cycling, and mountaineering should never be attempted when under the influence of mind-altering substances.

Sometimes, people get lost in the most seemingly benign circumstances. There have been instances where people have gotten lost going to the bathroom. They crawled out of their tent in the middle of the night without a headlamp, wandered into the woods, got turned around in the dark, and were unable to find their way back to their tent until daybreak.

Play it smart and pack the holy trinity every time you head into the outdoors: a sharp knife, rope or cord, and something you can use to light a fire, such as matches or a firestarter.

WHAT TO CARRY WHEN YOU GO HIKING

There's a saying in the outdoor survivalist community: the more you know, the less you carry. The idea is that the more knowledge you gain about how to survive in the outdoors, the more freedom you have to leave some gear at home. For example, if you know how to set up a shelter using a tarp and cord (and you don't mind increasing your exposure to the elements), you can opt to leave your tent behind.

That being said, there is certain gear that should never be left at home. However experienced you may be in the outdoors, you should never leave behind the ten essentials (see page 33). And even navigation experts should carry a compass and a map. Some survivalists claim that you only need to carry the holy trinity: a knife, a fire-starting implement (matches or a lighter), and some cord or rope. However, most outdoor experts would argue that, regardless of your wilderness expertise, the following ten essentials list is the bare minimum:

66 The more you know, the less you carry. 99

- **Navigation:** compass, map, GPS device (optional)
- **Light:** headlamp or flashlight
- **Sun protection:** sunscreen, sunglasses, sun-protective clothing
- **First aid:** medical kit, prescription medications, and insect repellent
- **Knife:** pocketknife and multi-tool (optional)
- **Fire:** matches, lighter, firestarters
- **Shelter:** tent or tarp
- **Extra food:** enough food to sustain you for an extra day
- **Extra water:** enough water to sustain you for an extra day and a water filtration device
- **Extra clothes:** bring layers for all types of weather

BAD HABITS THAT GET PEOPLE LOST

Sometimes "getting lost" is a state of mind, in a sense. You may not even be that off course when you get a gut feeling that something is amiss. Hiking along nonchalantly, you realize you're not quite sure where you are. But you keep going. You look around, perhaps pause,

MISLEADING MAPS

A good map is key to avoid getting lost. But not all maps are equally reliable. Many ancient maps depicted monsters and fantastical creatures. These illustrations would spark curiosity, sometimes provoking further exploration in distant lands to confirm or deny the legends. One such map, of the Patagonia region of Argentina created in 1562, was illustrated with giants, leading to the long-standing belief that a nine-foot-tall race of humans resided in the southernmost tip of South America. Explorers would continue to "see" giants in this part of the world for another two hundred years.

In the early years of mapmaking, some parts of the world were drawn with such inaccuracy that well-known landmarks were barely recognizable. For instance, an early Spanish explorer drew a map showing California surrounded on all sides by ocean—likely the result of confusing it with the Baja Peninsula. However, this mistake led to California being drawn as an island for the next few hundred years.

When Columbus sailed to America, he was actually aiming for Asia, but he was going off of an old map created by Ptolemy, the father of geography and realistic cartography. Ptolemy's map of the world showed the earth as 30 percent smaller than it actually is, and used Arabian miles for its scale, which were longer than the Italian miles Columbus was used to. As a result, Columbus thought his destination would be much closer than it was.

A Spanish map created in 1539 showed an island called Bermeja off the coast of the Yucatán Peninsula. The Mexican government started searching for the island in the 1990s, hoping to secure rights to any oil there. The search was finally called off in 2009, when a group of explorers determined that the island did not exist.

Perhaps one of the most fatal maps in the history of mapmaking is the con that Scottish adventurer Gregor MacGregor pulled off in 1822, with his wildly romantic claims about a new Central American utopia named Poyais that he was going to rule. Traveling to London, he persuaded hundreds of investors to purchase government bonds and land certificates. But when British settlers ventured to the coordinates that MacGregor had listed, all they found was a swamp. Of the 270 colonists who made the journey, more than half died.

look back. At some point, you finally wonder "where am I?" or "why is the sun setting in the east?"

Because two heads are better than one, it's a lot better to get lost with a group than by yourself. If you put everyone's strengths together, there will hopefully be enough communal know-how to determine where the group went astray, and how to get back on track. When hiking or traveling in groups, it's a good idea to designate someone as the keeper of the map, compass, and GPS device. This way, one person will take responsibility for route-finding, rather than everyone assuming that someone else is handling it. However, the map should be stored in an accessible location (such as near the outside of someone's backpack) so that anyone in the group can take a look when necessary. As a preventive measure, it's always a good idea to let someone know when you will be venturing into the wild and to share the trail you plan to follow *before* you set out. If worse comes to worst, this allows search and rescue teams to narrow their search area and find you quickly.

Designating a map keeper doesn't mean that other members of the group are off the hook. Everyone should try to stay alert to their surroundings. This way, everyone's cumulative observations can be used to keep the group on course.

Many modern people are so used to noises and distractions that the relative silence of the outdoors makes them uncomfortable. Perhaps for this reason, some break the silence by playing music. These

> **"The key point is to STOP: stop, think, observe, and plan. If you're lost, you need to avoid getting more lost."**

technological devices take our attention away from the details of the trail: smells and sounds, temperature and terrain changes. Taking note of these details is part of the art of awareness.

One technological device that may be worth bringing is your smartphone. If you can get a signal, you may be able to simply call someone and let them know you're lost and need assistance. If you have maps downloaded to your phone, you can use your phone's GPS to plot a course out. Even without a signal, most smartphones have a built-in compass, which can be used to help regain a sense of direction.

Some people panic when they realize they're turned around. They will actually set down their pack (with all their gear), and roam off to try and find the road they know is just beyond the edge of the forest—except, they don't find that forest edge, or their way back to their pack.

STOP WHEN YOU REALIZE YOU'RE LOST

A common piece of advice when you get turned around in the woods is to stop and hug a tree. While this won't help you find your way, the key point is to STOP: stop, think, observe, and plan. If you're lost, you need to avoid getting more lost. Hugging a tree helps to keep you from wandering farther away from where you want to be.

Stop: Quit moving. Sit down. Hug a tree if need be. Yes, you're on the verge of panic but you only have one goal now: to get un-lost and survive.

Think: OK, now that you've stopped, think over your situation. Ask yourself the following questions:

- Are you on the trail?
- Were there turns in the trail?
- Were there signs that you remember seeing, but didn't pay attention to?
- When was the last time you were sure you were headed in the right direction?
- Could you backtrack by following your own tracks?

EMERGENCY COMMUNICATION DEVICES

Personal emergency communication devices are good to have on hand for peace of mind. ResQLink, SPOT, and inReach are different brands, but they all serve the same function: a button that allows you to contact a search and rescue organization. The devices work even when you're out of cell range to transmit and then send your GPS location. Some devices include features like a satellite-enabled text messaging function, or a GPS mapping capability that allows you to track your path and email those coordinates to loved ones.

If the price tags on these devices feel cost prohibitive, search for used options online. Many people will buy emergency communication devices for a single trip and then sell them in good condition at more affordable rates.

- If you were with other people, how long ago was it that you parted ways? (Sometimes backtracking to where you and another person diverged can help you reorient.)

Observe: Hopefully, you're a bit calmer now. Start looking in all directions while staying by your tree. Is there anything you can see back beyond where you came from? Do you notice any distant landmarks or landscape features, such as a high peak or a water tower?

Is it possible to climb the tree you're sitting under so you can get a better view of your terrain? Were there any sounds that you recall from earlier, such as the rush of water from a river, or the buzz of insects, or even the sound of cars on a distant road? Try closing your

> **If you're lost, confused, uncertain, or mixed-up, moving will just get you more confused. If you're operating out of fear or panic, your decisions will not be your best. Stop, breathe, and think.**

eyes, cupping your hand behind your ear to amplify the sound, and listening. Slowly, turn a bit and listen again. Turn some more. Do you hear anything different, new, or familiar?

Plan: It was good that you stopped, and breathed, and attempted to take stock of your surroundings. Now, what are you going to do? You could just stay there, and try to make yourself more visible. If it's safe, a smoky fire is a good way to make yourself more visible to others, including rescuers. If it's getting cold, a good shelter may help you get through the night.

You should only push on if you have a fairly good idea of where you need to go and you have plenty of daylight left. But if you have collected enough facts to try and find your way out, pull out a notepad and pen and make yourself a map. It's also important to find a way to leave some sort of trail or sign of your path, in case someone is attempting to find you. If you are even somewhat doubtful about your ability to find your way back, call an emergency search and rescue (SAR) team on your cell phone, or satellite emergency communication device—ResQLink, SPOT, or inReach—if you are out of range. In these cases, it is imperative that you stay where you are and not travel any farther. This is because SAR teams will start their search at the last place they can confirm that you were, what they refer to as PLS or Point Last Seen. So, the farther you are from your starting point, the greater the distance the SAR team will have to search, and the longer it may take them to find you. If you can leave concrete clues as to the path you have taken, this will help the SAR team narrow down

SEND IN THE HOUNDS

Some SAR teams employ dogs to aid them in their search. The bloodhound, perhaps the most iconic tracking dog, uses its unique physiological makeup to sleuth out the whereabouts of lost humans. Gifted with about 230 million scent receptors—forty times that of humans—bloodhounds quickly form "scent memories" more detailed to them than photographs are to humans. Their unique folds and long ears help funnel scents to their nose and keep them on track. Bloodhounds are very persistent, and have been known to hold to trails for nearly 150 miles in search of their subject. Suffice it to say, if you had the nose of a bloodhound, you wouldn't need a map!

their search area. In SAR lingo, LKP or Last Known Position can be determined by clues left by you deliberately, such words spelled out in stones or sticks or written in the dirt, or by inadvertent clues such as shoe prints or broken branches.

Don't panic: Yes, easy to say, harder to do. If you're lost, confused, uncertain, or mixed-up, moving will just get you more confused. If you're operating out of fear or panic, your decisions will not be your best. This is because in times of stress, the prefrontal cortex, or the thinking or logic part of your brain, shuts down. Instead, the amygdala, or the lizard part of your brain, takes over. It sounds an alarm to the control center in your brain, and profound physical reactions ensue. Your body floods with adrenaline (that's why your heart is pounding!) and your breathing quickens. Your digestion and other nonessential functions shut down, and your body concentrates on powering your large muscles. This stress response is meant to allow you to flee an attacking animal, fight off a foe, or dodge a falling tree. However, you are lost, not under attack, and you need your thinking brain the most.

Instead of panicking, stop and take some deep breaths. Breathing helps re-center you and your brain, and allows your prefrontal cortex to regain control. You'll feel calmer and make better decisions. Focus on solutions, and stay positive.

3

Natural Observations

— ✕ —

Learning the Lay of the Land

> *"The ability to observe, and the ability to see the little things that seem trivial at first, may become amazingly important and meaningful."*
>
> Harold Gatty

L earning to read nature's signs is an important skill to help avoid getting lost. While there is no *single* natural sign that will always tell you which direction to travel, by practicing observing and understanding a range of features, along with using your common sense and thinking on your feet, you'll have a good chance of determining compass points and knowing how to find your way around without modern devices. Here are a few general guidelines to get you started.

STUDY THE LAY OF THE LAND

The best way to understand the landscape you're in is to find a high spot where you can observe as much of the local terrain as possible. Whether it's hiking to the top of a rocky peak or climbing a tree, seek out an elevated area with an unimpeded view of the terrain.

Look for the flat zones, signs of water, the high peaks, the undulating valleys—anything relevant to your ability to travel and obtain

SIGNS IN NATURE THAT ARE MISLEADING

Does moss really grow on the north side of trees? It often does, since the northern side of trees tends to have more shade, creating the cool, moist conditions that are ideal for moss. But that's in the Northern Hemisphere. In the Southern Hemisphere, the shade is on the southern side of trees. And the reality is that moss can grow on any side of a tree that provides the optimal conditions for moss to thrive.

Should you follow birds to find water? No. Birds have unpredictable flight patterns when it comes to their aerial searches for food and water, so they should never be followed in hopes of finding a water source.

water. Jot down your observations in a notebook, especially if it's your first time in a new area.

It's important to know the location of any body of water you might have to cross. Plan to go around, or cross where the water is either narrowest (and you can build a makeshift bridge), or the most shallow.

USING TREES

When using trees to orient yourself, one general rule is that trees tend to be warmer on the south side and cooler on the north side. Another is that if you encounter a tree stump that has been neatly cut, the side where the rings are wider is most likely the north to northeast side of the tree. The bark might also be thicker on the north and northeastern sides.

The tip of a tree may also be a clue as to your orientation. If you know the most common pattern of the prevailing local winds, you can note which direction the tops of trees are pointing or leaning. If many of the trees along a ridgeline point in the same direction, and

The tips of trees lean in the direction of prevailing winds. If you know the direction the wind blows most often, the tree tips will helpfully point you in that same direction.

the local prevailing wind often comes from the southwest, then the tops of the trees likely are pointing toward the northeast.

The tips of pines and hemlocks, typically found at higher elevations, often point east, the direction of prevailing winds. Again, the operative word here is "often," not "always."

The type of tree can also tell you something about where you are. Isolated deciduous trees tend to show the heaviest growth toward the south—where they receive the most sunlight. A river can sometimes be located by keeping an eye out for a stand of willows or alders—particularly useful if a river is a landmark you're trying to navigate toward.

The graceful arching branches of a willow tree indicate a good water source is nearby.

OTHER PLANT OBSERVATIONS

Plants have long been used for general orientation. For instance, the leaves of prickly lettuce seem to fold up vertically, especially when it is very hot, so that the flat edge of the leaf faces the sun. The edges of the leaves often follow the sun across the sky, earning it the nickname "compass plant." Though other plants share this nickname, prickly lettuce is one of the most reliable for orienting toward the cardinal directions.

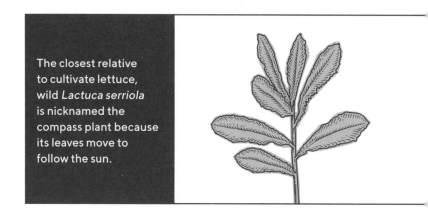

The closest relative to cultivate lettuce, wild *Lactuca serriola* is nicknamed the compass plant because its leaves move to follow the sun.

Keep in mind that "south" in these cases includes anywhere from southeast to southwest, nearly a full 180 degrees of the horizon. That's certainly helpful if you're completely lost, but a compass plant is not a compass!

Flowers often face the sun—this is where sunflowers got their name. By pointing a time-lapse camera at a sunflower, you can watch it turn as the sun moves across the sky throughout the day. If you already have a good idea which direction south is, you can observe nearby flowers to see if they're facing the direction you guessed.

Goldenrods, of which there are several species nationwide, have long been used as a direction finder, as the tips of the nodding flower

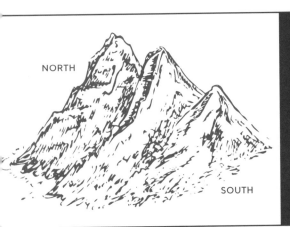

NORTH

SOUTH

If you are on a slope, pay attention to the type of flora around you. Southern exposures receive more light, while northern exposures retain more moisture.

heads generally face north. To aid in navigation, it's best to observe them in open fields. In canyons, where there are local prevailing winds, the flowers will simply flow with the breeze. Similarly, the giant saguaro cactus of the southwest produces flowers in the summer at the tips of its giant "arms." These flowers, and the fruit that follows, tend to be more tightly clustered on the east side of the plant.

DRY GROUND VERSUS MOIST GROUND

Any hill or mountain range that spreads out in an east-west direction will retain more moisture on the northern side. The south side, which receives more sunlight, will have different plant communities and is generally drier. Because there is less direct sun on the northern half of these ranges during the winter, they will retain snow longer and have more shade, and thus more ferns, moss, and other moisture-loving plants.

So if you're hearing loud, dry crackles from the vegetation as you walk along an east-west range, you are probably on the southern side. Similarly, if it's very quiet, with ferns and moist leaves, then you might be on the northern drop. But you'd still need to make other observations to be certain.

SNOW MELT AND SHADOWS

If you're in snowed-in terrain with overcast skies, navigation can get very tricky. In these conditions, it can be easy to get turned around. So how can you ascertain directions once you get confused?

Start by observing the snow that has piled up at the base of trees, bushes, and other plants. If you look carefully and closely, and if the cloud cover is not too thick, you might see a slight shadow cast on the northern side of the plant. (This would not apply if you're in a dense forest.)

Also, if there has been any snowmelt at the base of trees or bushes, it will be the most obvious on the southern side.

These are just a few of the observations that can be made from the subtle clues that nature provides. If you want to get better at natural navigation, pay attention to everything that can safely be seen, smelled, touched, and heard.

4

The Sun, Moon, and Stars

—— ✕ ——

Celestial Navigation and
Seasonal Influences

*"When you follow a star you know you
will never reach that star; rather it will
guide you to where you want to go."*

Jeanette Winterson, *Boating for Beginners*

Observing trees, plants, and snow isn't the only way the natural world can help you get from here to there: the movement of the sun, the moon, and the stars can also be used to navigate.

A lot can be learned by simply observing the path of the sun throughout the year. All ancient civilizations studied the sun, and were well aware of how it travelled through the sky, and how this path changed from the winter solstice to the summer solstice. Today, many of us learn in childhood the basics of how the earth and the solar system operate. But ancient peoples did not have the advantage of textbooks or model globes that spin on their axis—they learned by direct observation, and then passed this information on through both oral tradition and in the orientation of key buildings and monuments.

The advantages of knowing the annual cycles of the sun and moon ranged from the mundane to the esoteric. The mundane included such tasks as basic navigation, telling the time or date, as well as knowing when to plant and harvest crops. On the esoteric side, the reasons included knowing the precise day to have an important ceremony, or to correspond with the days of the gods.

THE ECLIPTIC

The ecliptic is an imaginary plane that represents the path of the sun and the moon across the canopy of the sky, from east to west, throughout the year. At the winter solstice in the Northern Hemisphere, the ecliptic is tilted 23½ degrees below the celestial equator, which is a plane extending perpendicularly from the earth's equator. At the summer solstice, the ecliptic is tilted 23½ degrees above the celestial equator. This is what gives the Northern Hemisphere the longer days of summer and shorter days of winter.

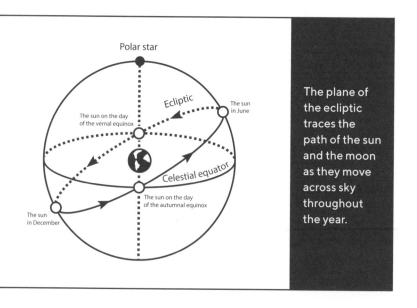

Polar star

The sun on the day of the vernal equinox

Ecliptic

The sun in June

Celestial equator

The sun on the day of the autumnal equinox

The sun in December

The plane of the ecliptic traces the path of the sun and the moon as they move across sky throughout the year.

Ancient people were aware of the angle of the ecliptic, and this knowledge was built into the mathematics governing many ancient monuments in North and South America, Ireland and India, in the stone circles of southern Africa, and many other places.

❝ Hand-railing is a form of very basic navigation using the ecliptic, or the path of the sun. This method involves keeping the sun to one side of your body, left or right, to help stay on a course. ❞

As the sun moves along the ecliptic, it goes through the twelve constellations of the zodiac. So once you learn to recognize the ecliptic, you'll start to recognize several familiar constellations, the names of which have come down to us over time. That's because people have seen images in, and then named, groupings of stars, like Leo the Lion, or Orion the Hunter, for thousands of years.

By 1930, astronomers worldwide decided to bring some order to our view of the sky. They determined the boundaries of eighty-eight constellations and gave them Latin names. Today, sky watchers and astronomers all use this accepted system.

USING THE SUN TO FIND YOUR WAY

Hand-railing is a form of very basic navigation using the ecliptic, or the path of the sun. This method involves keeping the sun to one side

ZODIAC CONSTELLATIONS

The twelve constellations located along the ecliptic that occupies 30 degrees celestial longitude are also the twelve signs of the zodiac used in astrology. These constellations are represented by different figures (animals and humans), occupying the path circling around the earth as it travels around the sun throughout the course of the year.

- **Capricorn (sea goat):** Best view in the Northern Hemisphere in August

- **Aquarius (water bearer):** Best viewed in the Northern Hemisphere in September

- **Pisces (fish):** Best viewed in the Northern Hemisphere in October

- **Aries (ram):** Best viewed in the Northern Hemisphere in November

- **Taurus (bull):** Best viewed in the Northern Hemisphere in December

- **Gemini (twins):** Best viewed in the Northern Hemisphere in January

- **Cancer (crab):** Best viewed in the Northern Hemisphere in February

- **Leo (lion):** Best viewed in the Northern Hemisphere in March

- **Virgo (virgin):** Best viewed in the Northern Hemisphere in April

- **Libra (scales):** Best viewed in the Northern Hemisphere in May

- **Scorpio (scorpion):** Best viewed in the Northern Hemisphere in June

- **Sagittarius (archer):** Best viewed in the Northern Hemisphere in July

Interestingly, while these signs have become symbolic for different birthdays, their corresponding constellation is not visible in the night sky during their designated zodiac calendar month.

of your body, left or right, to help stay on a course. For example, keeping the sun to your left enables you to walk in a consistently westerly direction. Or in the reverse case, if you need to walk in a consistently easterly direction, keep the sun to your right.

SEASONAL CHANGES IN THE SUN'S PATTERN

One of the most basic methods for using the sun to determine direction is to observe its position. But because of the angle of the sun in the sky changes with the seasons, the sun does not always rise in the same spot on the eastern horizon, or set in the same spot on the western horizon. In fact, the sun rises due east and sets due west only two days out of the year, which are called the equinoxes. As they say in the aviation industry, "Reaching your target is a constant series of minor corrections."

The earth has a tilt, which impacts the position of the sunrise and sunset as it revolves around the sun throughout the year. Around the summer solstice, the North Pole is at its closest point to the sun. This is why the poles experience such long days during the summer and such short days during the winter months, and why the sun will seem to rise and set north of due east in the North Pole during the summer. When using the sun for navigation, it's important to keep in mind what time of year it is and how that will impact the sun's position in the sky. For example, if you were to hike toward sunrise in March or September and then hike back toward sunset, you would likely arrive back at your starting location. In other words, you would have hiked due east, and then back due west. However, if you did the same thing in midwinter, hiking toward sunrise would take you northeast.

THE SOLAR COMPASS

A solar compass, also called a sun compass, assesses the position of the sun to help determine location. It is similar to a sundial in that it uses shadow to note cardinal direction. Usually, a solar compass is made with a flat disk or compass card, marked with degree units. The shadow cast onto the disk or card lines up with a degree, which indicates direction.

A solar compass is particularly useful at the poles, where the magnetic pull of high altitudes and, rarely, the earth's own magnetic pull renders magnetic compasses inaccurate. Since a solar compass isn't affected by magnetic fields, it is a fail-safe option for navigating near the poles.

OBSERVING A SHADOW

Using a solar compass is a good way to begin observing the path of the sun. You can start by creating a mechanism that serves as both a sundial and a sun compass. First, pound a stick solidly into the ground. Now put a pebble at the end of where the stick casts a shadow. Continue placing pebbles at the end of the shadow as it moves throughout the day.

The shadow will be the shortest around noon, when the sun is directly overhead (one o'clock in the afternoon if there is daylight saving time). If you draw a straight line from the stick to the stone marking the shortest shadow, you should have, more or less, a north-south line. A perpendicular line will then give you an east-west line,

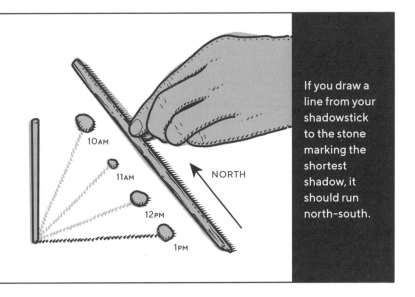

If you draw a line from your shadowstick to the stone marking the shortest shadow, it should run north-south.

10AM

11AM

NORTH

12PM

1PM

the beginning of a compass. This technique is most accurate around the summer solstice, when the days are of equal length.

If you know the approximate time of the sunrise and sunset, you can evenly divide the arc formed by the stones and create a crude, but usable, sundial clock. If you are camping out with friends, make this stick sundial large enough that everyone can easily see and refer to it during the day. Locate the sundial in the most open area, where it will receive sunlight throughout the entire day, with no interference from the shadows of trees.

These are the simple and easy steps to make your first solar compass, as well as a primitive clock. If you want something with even more accuracy, you'll need greater complexity.

DIY SUNDIAL

What you are making with your rocks and sticks is a crude version of an equatorial sundial.

DETERMINING HOW MUCH TIME (USABLE LIGHT) YOU HAVE BEFORE SUNSET

Let's say it's getting late in the day and you have to decide if you have time to get back to your car before dark or if you should set up camp. This is an old method for determining approximately how long it will be until the sun sets.

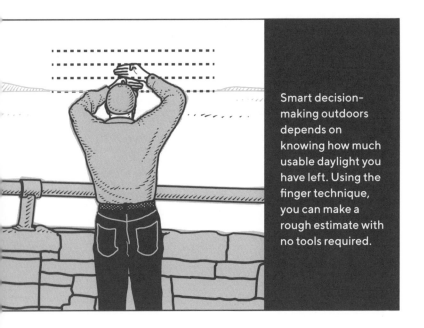

Smart decision-making outdoors depends on knowing how much usable daylight you have left. Using the finger technique, you can make a rough estimate with no tools required.

Face the horizon and extend your arm in front of you. Tuck in your thumb. Bend your hand so that your fingers are parallel to the horizon. If you cannot see the western horizon, stand erect and assume it is located where your eyes look out perpendicular from your body. Now, using your four fingers, measure up from the horizon to the sun. Each finger represents about fifteen minutes of the sun's travel across the sky.

Despite differences in finger size and arm length, this technique works pretty well for most people. You can check your own ability by consulting sunset tables in advance. Keep in mind that while in the summer, there will still be usable light for at least an hour after sundown, in the winter, it gets pretty dark very soon after the sun dips below the horizon.

USING YOUR ANALOG WATCH TO DETERMINE DIRECTIONS

This is an old technique that still has some relevance. Your analog watch can double as a compass, assuming it is keeping accurate time. In the Northern Hemisphere, hold your watch flat and point the hour hand at the sun. The halfway point between the hour hand and twelve will point south. If it's daylight saving time, it is the halfway point between the hour hand and one that will point south.

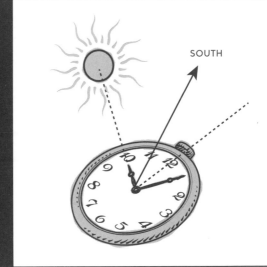

If you have an analog watch, use it as a compass. Point the hour hand at the sun. The halfway point between the twelve and the hour hand marks south.

SOUTH

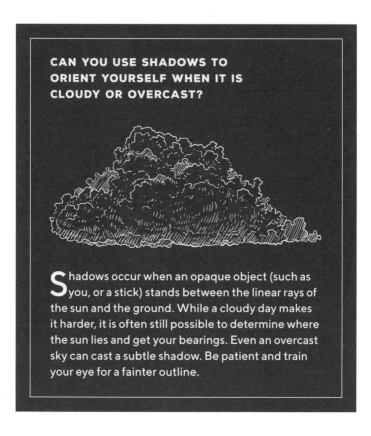

CAN YOU USE SHADOWS TO ORIENT YOURSELF WHEN IT IS CLOUDY OR OVERCAST?

Shadows occur when an opaque object (such as you, or a stick) stands between the linear rays of the sun and the ground. While a cloudy day makes it harder, it is often still possible to determine where the sun lies and get your bearings. Even an overcast sky can cast a subtle shadow. Be patient and train your eye for a fainter outline.

Here is a technique to try if the sun is obscured by clouds. Hold a match or twig vertically along the edge of the watch. Unless it's extremely overcast, you should be able to see at least a faint shadow. Turn the watch until the match's faint shadow falls directly on the hour hand. The hour hand is now pointing at the sun, and you can determine south.

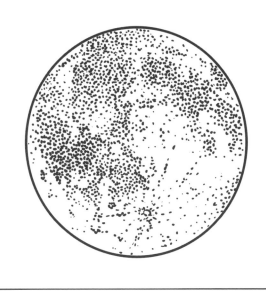

The full moon occurs when it is on the opposite side of Earth from the sun. That allows its face to be fully illuminated by the sun's light.

But don't most people have digital watches these days? This works just as well with a clockface that you draw on a piece of paper, again, assuming your digital watch is keeping correct time. Let's say your digital watch says it's three o'clock. Draw a round clock face on a piece of paper and write in at least the three and the twelve on the clock face. Hold that paper flat and point the three at the sun. The halfway point between the hour hand and twelve will point south.

NAVIGATING BY THE MOON

The moon is a good navigational guide when the constellations are too faint or obscured to clearly see the night sky. First, it helps to know that, like the sun, the moon rises in the east and sets in the west. By observing the position of the moon in the sky, you can also determine the time of night, which can orient you to the cardinal directions.

Because of the sun and moon's east-west trajectory, a crescent moon can literally point you in a southerly direction. From the top tip of the crescent, draw a line with your eyes straight down to the bottom tip, and then extend this line down to the horizon. In the Northern Hemisphere, the point where your line intersects with the horizon is a rough estimate of where south is. In the Southern Hemisphere, this is reversed. The point where this line intersects with the horizon can be used as north when wayfinding.

Using the reflection of the sun's light, a crescent moon can also be used to determine east and west. The bright side of the moon—or the part of the moon that is visible—will correlate to the position of the sun. If the sun hasn't yet set and the moon is rising in the east, the bright side of the crescent moon will be facing west. After midnight, the bright side of the moon will face east.

NAVIGATING BY THE STARS

Just as it is important to learn the observed path of the sun and moon, it is important to become familiar with the stars. It turns out the night sky holds many clues to cardinal directions.

UNDERSTANDING THE NIGHT SKY

First, go outside on a clear night and observe the stars. You may or may not know the constellations, or be able to recognize them. That's

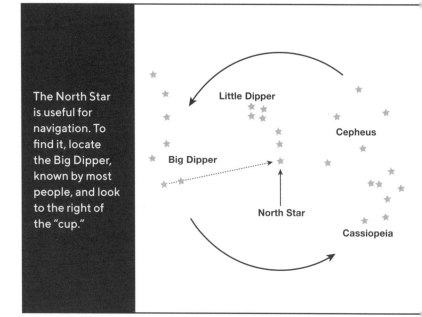

The North Star is useful for navigation. To find it, locate the Big Dipper, known by most people, and look to the right of the "cup."

Little Dipper

Cepheus

Big Dipper

North Star

Cassiopeia

okay for now. Just observe what you see, and attempt to take note of various patterns or shapes.

Go back outside an hour later. Referring to your notes or drawings, you'll notice that the stars are not in the same location as they were. What happened? Initially, you may think that the stars moved. However, what you are observing is the earth's revolution.

Now it's time to make more specific observations. Find a spot where you can see the stars in relation to a fixed point, such as the top of the neighbor's house or an odd treetop. Look for patterns, such as groups of stars that seem to form a triangle, a square, or even a line.

Now, come back in an hour, locate your fixed point, and look for those same stars. Note whether they have moved right or left, up or down, since knowing how the stars appear to rotate in the sky can be helpful in determining general directions.

You can follow up on what you've learned with the following quick and dirty guide to astronomy, another valuable way to gain a basic understanding of the movement of the stars.

THE CONSTELLATIONS

According to the International Astronomical Union, the governing body of the stars, there are eighty-eight official constellations. No, you do not need to memorize the star charts for all eighty-eight in order to use them as a guide. Knowing the formation and behavior patterns of just a few key constellations and stars can aid enormously in navigation.

GETTING TO KNOW THE NORTH STAR (POLARIS)

The North Star is the brightest star in the sky. True or false? Ask this to an average group of people, and most would say yes. In reality, it is not. But it shines brightly in other ways.

While the Dog Star holds the distinction as the brightest star in the sky, the North Star is highly significant for using the sky for wayfinding. Since the North Star is always vertically aligned with the North Pole, once you locate the North Star, you know which direction is north. Not only that, but it serves as a fixed point by which to track the patterns of other constellations and stars. If you were to

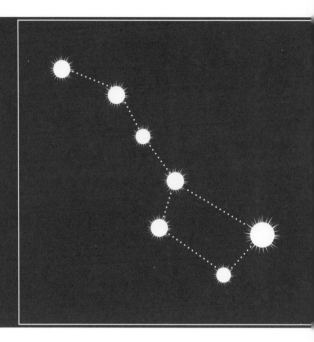

One of the most recognizable shapes in the night sky, the Big Dipper is formed by seven stars, with three forming the handle and four the "bowl" or cup of the dipper.

watch it with time-lapse photography (or even over several hours with the naked eye), the North Star would appear to be stationary with all the stars rotating counterclockwise around it. What this perceived movement is really capturing is the rotation of the earth, but even so, the movement patterns can also give you important information about the cardinal directions.

You can practice locating the North Star by going outside on a clear night and facing north. If you live in a rural area, there may be so many visible stars that it could be hard to make out distinct constellations. You might even see the Milky Way. If you live near

THE GREAT BEAR

What we call the Big Dipper is just a part of the larger constellation known as the Great Bear, or Ursa Major. The handle of the dipper is the tail of the great bear. Ursa Major is probably the most widely known constellation, going back to ancient times. Ancient peoples saw this big bear, rotating forever around the middle of the sky, and told countless stories and myths about it.

or in an urban area, on the other hand, you're only going to see the brightest stars. This is because light pollution from the city obscures the fainter ones.

If you're not sure which of the stars you see is the North Star, a good place to start is by locating the Big Dipper, one of the easiest star formations for most people to recognize and usually visible in both rural and urban areas. In this combination of seven stars, three stars appear in a line forming the handle while four stars make up the cup of what ancients peoples saw as a large water dipper (or a ladle, in modern times).

Once you've located the Big Dipper, trace along the formation until you reach the right edge of the "cup." Then look to the right and see if you can spot the North Star. If you still need more help, take note of the distance between the two stars forming the right

Without any navigation instruments, you can determine your latitude by using the North Star and your fist.

Once you've located the North Star, draw an imaginary line from it to the horizon. Extend your arm toward this intersecting point, make a fist with your knuckles facing the horizon, and place it at the horizon line. Then, make a fist with your other hand and place it on top of your extended fist. Alternating hands, count how many fists it takes to reach the North Star. Though everyone's hand size varies, the average size approximately translates to 10 degrees. So, for example, if the distance between the horizon and the North Star measures four fists, your latitude is approximately 40 degrees north.

edge of the cup. The North Star is approximately five times that distance to the right. It should now be recognizable to you.

Once you've located the Big Dipper and the North Star, note their location. Then, in an hour, come back to the spot where you had been observing them. You'll notice that the earth has rotated. The North Star still appears to be in pretty much the same location, but the Big Dipper will have rotated counterclockwise 15 degrees in the sky. Come back in another hour, and the Big Dipper will have rotated

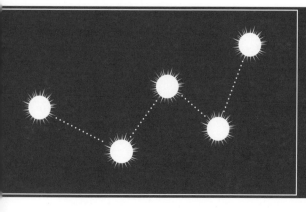

Casseopeia can be found roughly the same distance from the North Star as the Big Dipper, just on the opposite side.

another 15 degrees. You're now witnessing the great twenty-four-hour "clockface" of the sky, with the North Star smack in the middle.

Now you know how to find north at night, assuming there aren't any clouds. (We're also assuming that you're north of the equator. At the equator, you won't see the North Star at all, because it will be right on the horizon. And if you live in the Southern Hemisphere . . . well, let's just say that the rest of this chapter won't have much relevance to you.)

If you know north, you obviously know south, and perpendicular to your imaginary north-south line is east and west. So, if you can find the North Star in the Northern Hemisphere, you will know all your cardinal points!

USING CASSIOPEIA TO FIND THE NORTH STAR

Cassiopeia is located on the opposite side of the North Star from the Big Dipper. Cassiopeia was a queen in Greek mythology, and ancient

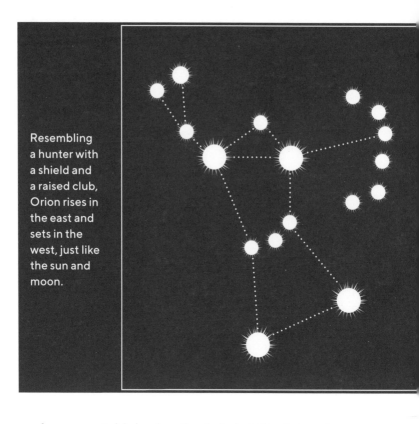

Resembling a hunter with a shield and a raised club, Orion rises in the east and sets in the west, just like the sun and moon.

people saw a seated lady when they looked at this cluster of stars. Some people also call this constellation the big M or big W, which more accurately describes the basic shape of the brightest stars of the constellation.

If you spot Cassiopeia, you can spot the North Star. Cassiopeia is found roughly the same distance away from the North Star as the Big Dipper, and roughly on the opposite side. So, Cassiopeia also rotates counterclockwise around the North Star, but roughly 180 degrees away from the Big Dipper.

GETTING TO KNOW ORION

Orion is an easy to recognize constellation, probably the most widely known celestial formation after the Big Dipper. Orion is said to resemble a hunter, with a shield, and a raised club. Four conspicuous stars provide a general outline for his body, and three stars in a line define his belt. From his belt hangs his sword. Below him is his dog, in the Big Dog constellation (Canis Major) with the star Sirius, or the Dog Star, being the brightest in the sky.

Orion is easily spotted, and the constellation travels just to the south of the ecliptic. This means that, roughly speaking, Orion rises in the east and sets in the west, just like the sun and moon. If you're lost and you can see Orion, you might be able to reorient yourself.

A SEMI-CLOUDY NIGHT

You're now aware that all stars appear to rotate counterclockwise around the North Star. But what if the night is a bit cloudy, with just a few stars visible here and there. How can you determine directions?

From a fixed location, begin to observe the stars you are able to see. This could be a bit challenging, because the clouds may be moving. Try to find stars unobscured by clouds and watch them over time to see what direction they are moving. If the stars appear to be rising, you are facing east. If the stars appear to be dropping in the sky, you're facing west. If you can mentally visualize all the stars,

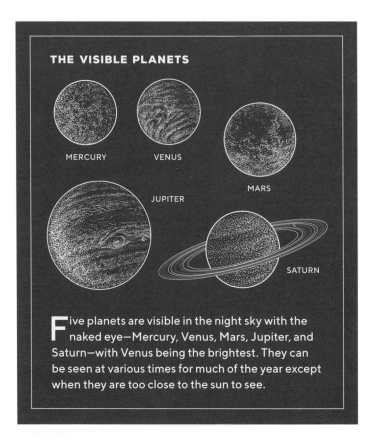

THE VISIBLE PLANETS

MERCURY

VENUS

MARS

JUPITER

SATURN

Five planets are visible in the night sky with the naked eye—Mercury, Venus, Mars, Jupiter, and Saturn—with Venus being the brightest. They can be seen at various times for much of the year except when they are too close to the sun to see.

slowly rotating counterclockwise around the North Star, this makes perfect sense.

If you're looking to the south, the stars will appear to be moving to the right, parallel to the horizon. Looking to the north makes this

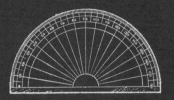

WHAT IS A PROTRACTOR?

A protractor may have been something you used as a kid to draw angles in school. It is also a useful instrument for measuring degrees in navigation, plotting a route on a map, and noting the angle of the stars in the sky.

A protractor is a circular or semicircular tool marked with 180 degrees (if semicircular) or 360 degrees (if circular). If you have a protractor, take a look to see if the degrees are set in one- or five-degree increments. Some protractors are even divvied up into four 90-degree quadrants rather than degrees, which limits the precision of the tool when using it for navigation.

In the Northern Hemisphere, the North Star will always appear in the sky as the same height above the horizon as your latitude. That means if I live 34 degrees above the equator, I can measure 34 degrees above the horizon with a protractor in order to try and locate the North Star. You can also use a protractor to see how high the North Star is above the horizon where you live. That angle equals your latitude.

a bit challenging. The stars above the North Star will appear to be moving to your left. However, if the patch of stars you're looking at is beneath the North Star, they will be drifting to the right.

As long as you grasp the fact that all the stars appear to rotate counterclockwise around the North Star, you'll be able to watch their movement over the course of an hour or so, and use that information to determine your cardinal directions.

5

The Map

—— × ——

Geography, Topography,
and Points of Interest

> *"If geography is prose,*
> *maps are iconography."*

Lennart Meri

Ancient peoples had only the sun, moon, stars, and natural surroundings to help them find their way. We can still use these methods to help us get from here to there, but now we can also use more accurate tools to help show us the way. A map is one such tool. It is an aerial picture of a specific area of terrain that shows the location of roads, buildings, towns, railroad lines, water, mines—everything you need to know if you are traveling through that area. Some maps focus on a particular feature that can help to smooth the user's journey.

ROAD MAPS

There are several types of road maps. You can purchase a map that shows major highways and interstate routes for traveling across the country, as well as regional maps for areas like the northwest or a specific state. These maps are produced by private map-making companies and also auto clubs. These maps are great while you're traveling in your car and staying on the highways, but not much help if you're traveling off-road.

GEOLOGICAL MAPS

The United States Geological Survey (USGS) and the bureau's state partners produce these maps that depict earthquake faults, and the dominant minerals found in a given area. They are great for geologists, geology students, and miners. Unless you are a highly specialized outdoor enthusiast, these are not likely to be the most useful maps for you.

TRAIL MAPS

Hiking, mountain biking, and trail riding are very popular and there are trail maps for each of these activities. If you plan to hike the Pacific Crest Trail, for example, you can get a whole book of maps that tells you not only where the trails are, but also where to camp, where to get water, and where stores and lodging are located.

The internet is a good source for doublechecking a map's accuracy in terms of closed trails or campsites, for example. You can source maps through regional nonprofit organizations, such as the Appalachian Trail Club or The Mountaineers, through the US National Park Service, especially good for trails near or around national parks, as well as through state and city agencies. Private publishers also put out books of trail maps along with recommendations.

FLIGHT PATHS

The maps used by pilots show the flight paths they need to follow to get from point A to point B. Commonly known as aeronautical charts, these are highly specialized maps whose data is provided and governed by the Federal Aviation Administration. Still of incredible importance to pilots, especially those flying by visual flight rules, these maps or charts are unlikely to be of value to a hiker or motorist.

LOCAL SPECIAL INTEREST MAPS

Any privately made map that depicts the layout of a particular area, such as a farm, a large zoo, an extensive campsite, or even Disneyland, is a special interest map. One type of special interest map that has gained popularity in recent years is the walking tour map. It is designed so that tourists can follow a preset route without a guide through special interest areas such as historic downtowns, public art displays, or environmental sanctuaries. As these private venues can contain different trails and routes within their boundaries, these maps can prove useful on day excursions.

MAP LEGENDS

Even if a map seems straightforward, be sure to read the map's legend before using it. Once, I was trying to find a lake that was marked on the map as being in the northeast corner of a large botanical garden. I was unable to find it until I realized that the legend noted that south was at the top of the map.

TOPOGRAPHIC MAPS

Because they are most useful to hikers and outdoor enthusiasts, in this chapter, we're going to focus on topographic maps. These maps illustrate everything you need to know about the terrain you're walking

Knowing how to recognize common map codes will ease your understanding of topographic maps and help you find your way.

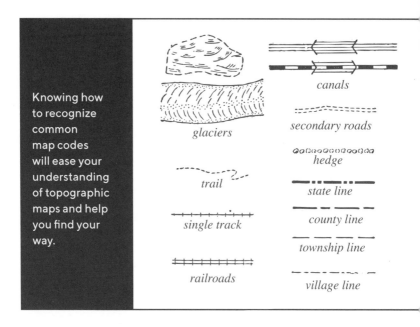

canals

secondary roads

hedge

state line

county line

township line

village line

glaciers

trail

single track

railroads

in, including rivers and springs, rises and falls in elevation, remote buildings, railroad lines, aqueducts, and, of course, roads, freeways, and other pieces of urban infrastructure. Topographic maps can both keep you on course and also help you choose the easiest route (which is not necessarily the shortest) between two points.

The first step is to purchase a topographic map for your territory. Note the year your topographic map was made before buying. Not all maps are updated annually, and some may be ten or twenty years old—meaning the world could have changed significantly from what's pictured. You also may want to check online for seasonal closures such as washed out trails or campsites closed due to forest fires.

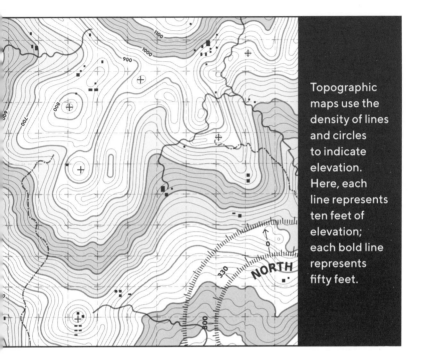

Topographic maps use the density of lines and circles to indicate elevation. Here, each line represents ten feet of elevation; each bold line represents fifty feet.

SYMBOLS AND COLORS ON TOPOGRAPHIC MAPS

The color coding is standardized for all topographic maps.

- Brown is used for contour lines.
- Blue signifies a water feature, like a river, lake, or stream.
- Green is vegetation.
- Black lines represent human-made features, such as water towers, buildings, power lines, roads, or trails.

- Red typically indicates major highways.
- Magenta/purple are revisions made to the map from previous versions.

Many similar objects with the same color are depicted in varying ways to differentiate them. For instance; whereas a solid blue line represents water that typically runs year-round, a dashed blue line is used to signify a seasonal stream. A single row of dashed black lines represents a trail, while two parallel dashed lines shows a dirt road wide enough for a vehicle. It is important to know what map symbols mean so you can understand what the actual terrain will look like from the map. Once you understand the codes and symbols that map-makers use, you'll be able to spot rivers, mines, campgrounds, gravel pits, archaeological sites, forest stations, and much more.

Here are some of the most common map symbols as a reference. You can also find a list of map symbols from the USGS.

CONTOUR LINES

A topographic map depicts changes in elevation that you would not see on a typical road map. The contour of the landscape is depicted by brown lines that are more or less parallel. These represent a set change in elevation, and each map will indicate the elevation change between the lines. At the bottom of the map, you'll read something like "contour interval 40 feet." A topographic map will also show the actual elevation above sea level at measured points. Larger or smaller distances between lines shows the flatness or steepness of the landscape. Where the lines are far apart, the landscape is nearly flat, such as a desert. Where you see lines tightly bunched together, you should be visualizing steep hillsides.

Study the map until you can visualize the rise and fall of the terrain. Note that rivers are at low points, with hills typically rising above them. The very top of a hill might be designated by a topographic line that is in the shape of an oval or circle. Peaks often appear as concentric rings that are close together. Ridges can be located on the map by looking for areas where the topographic lines are close together on one side of a land feature, but more spread out on the other.

Having a practical understanding of topographic lines is useful when planning a route of travel. While it's easy to chart a straight line on a map, it might be difficult to travel on if the line is constantly crossing topographic lines, going up and over hills. If you want the *easiest* route from your point to your destination, then you should chart a course that allows you to *stay within the map's topographic lines* as much as possible. That's because a course that stays within the same topographic lines will have minimal elevation gain or loss.

SCALE OF THE MAP

Below are the three most commonly used scales for topographic maps, but in general, the bigger the number, the more territory is covered on the map.

- **1:250,000 map:** This scale means that one inch on the map represents 250,000 inches, or approximately four miles, of

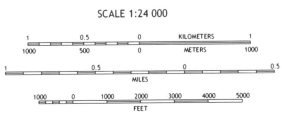

Scale allows you to see the relative sizes of features and distances in a large area.

SCALE 1:24 000

CONTOUR INTERVAL 10 FEET
NORTH AMERICAN VERTICAL DATUM OF 1988

territory. A map like this gives you the broadest view of your terrain, and usually covers a distance of about one hundred miles.

- **1:62,500 map:** This scale means that one map inch translates to 62,500 inches, or about one mile, in the field.
- **1:24,000 map (a.k.a., a 7.5 minute map):** This is one of the most commonly used maps in the United States. On this scale, one map inch equals 24,000 inches, or two thousand feet.

The smaller the scale, the more detail is covered. Think of this as zooming in with your camera. The more you zoom in, the more detail will come into focus, but the smaller the area that fills the frame.

ALIGNING YOUR MAP WITHOUT A COMPASS

You can get to a destination with just your topographic map, as long as it is aligned with the terrain. Start by laying your map on a flat surface. Then it's time to align true north on your map with true north in your environment. Remember, true north (a.k.a. grid north) is usually at the top of your map (but check the legend to confirm). While it is best to determine true north using a compass, if you do not have one, you can use a solar compass as described in chapter four. Remember, this is not one hundred percent accurate—your "north" may be off by a few or many degrees.

Another way to find north is through visual alignment. This requires you to be in an area that is high enough, or clear enough, that you can see many obvious landmarks in at least three directions, preferably more. On your map, select a significant landmark, such as a water tower, that is within your sight. Turn your map so that a pencil line drawn between where you think you are to the water tower will continue in a straight line to the actual location of the water tower. Next, look directly behind you and look for another significant geographic feature, such as the top of a peak. Locate the peak on the map. Adjust the orientation of your map so that a straight line from where you think you are on the map, to the peak, continues to the actual peak. Continue looking at dominant landmarks in all directions, and make slight adjustments to your map so that the orientation reflects the actual terrain around you. Now, look at the cardinal directions on the map. Look up to see which direction you have to stand to face north. Place a few rocks on the map so its orientation is secured.

USING YOUR MAP TO GET SOMEWHERE

Study the map that you've aligned with the surrounding terrain and note where the roads and trails go. Remember, a map gives

Once you know the direction you need to go, use trees as living "pins" in your topography to visualize your way.

you a bird's-eye view of the terrain. It tells you what's behind say, a hill, important information if you don't have a clear view from your vantage point. Consider whether your proposed path crosses elevations lines. Staying within the lines means your journey will be more level.

Let's say you want to get to a small campground with a little stream. It's located about halfway across the map distance from your current location, and exactly at a 90-degree angle. You know it's 90 degrees because it's in a horizontal line exactly to the right, or east, of where you're located.

The easiest way to get there is to look along the line on your map from where you are to where you want to go and extend it to the east. This is best accomplished by lining up two trees in a straight line with your current location and your intended location.

Once you have your imaginary line, follow it to the first tree. Once you reach the first tree, line up two more trees and do the same thing. Remember, once you pick up your map and start walking, it becomes less and less useful until you stop and realign it visually with the terrain.

If everything goes well, you should arrive at the campground. How long it will take you is another question.

KNOWING YOUR PACE

To know how long it will take to reach the campground, you need to know two things: the scale of the map and your own pace. You can easily determine the scale of the map by checking the measurement icon, typically located on the bottom. In terms of knowing

❝ Pacing is a skill worth knowing. Many soldiers from both Vietnam and the Middle East have reported that keeping track of their paces was a key factor in their general navigation. ❞

your pace, this is something you should determine before setting out. At home, go to a place where you know the distance between a starting point and an ending point. This could be a football field, or you can just take a measuring tape and measure out a distance on

FACTORS THAT AFFECT PACING

In the US armed forces, a pace as a unit of measurement is generally considered to be 22 to 30 inches long. For navigation purposes, what's important to know is the length of *your* pace.

Additionally, there are several factors that must be taken into account when using pacing as a method to gauge time and distance. These are the most common:

WEATHER AND ELEMENTS: Walking over snow or ice or ground made slippery by rain causes you to move more slowly and with shorter paces.

WIND: A good tailwind at your back can quicken your pace, while a strong headwind does the opposite.

INCLINE AND GRADE: Pace counts can be affected dramatically by slopes, quickening going down hills and slowing going up.

ATTIRE: Both your shoes and the relative comfort and weight of your clothing and pack can affect your speed and the length of your stride.

SURFACE MATERIAL: It's slow going in thick mud, deep snow, or in loose sand.

VISIBILITY: Fog, driving rain, or falling light can all slow you down.

flat ground. A good minimum distance for determining your pace is one hundred feet.

At the starting point, step forward with one foot and then the other, walking at a normal pace. Each step you take counts as one pace. Continue this way for the full one hundred feet, noting how many paces you made and how long it took (using a timer). Repeat the process two more times, then add the three totals together, and divide by three to get the average. Let's say it took you an average of twenty seconds and twenty paces to cover one hundred feet.

If your destination is two miles away on your map, the rest is simple math. A mile is 5,280 feet. So, to calculate your estimated travel time to walk two miles, you would multiply 5,280 (feet) by 2 (miles), which is 10,560 total feet. Then, you would divide this by 100 (feet), which is 105.6. Next, you would multiply 105.6 by 20 (the number of seconds it takes you to walk 100 feet). This comes out to 2,112 seconds, which when divided by 60, equals 35.2, or about 35 minutes. So, walking your average pace, it will take you approximately 35 minutes to reach the campground.

The above is a good starting point, but remember that the number of paces and the time it takes you will change as the terrain changes. Most people will speed up with longer strides on downhills while slowing and shortening their pace as they move uphill, carry heavy loads, or encounter significant brush. Walking in the wilds for any distance, which often involves navigating obstacles, hills, and fatigue, will also impact the accuracy of your pace count.

Pacing is most useful at shorter distances—the longer the distance you are traveling, the more variables there are (including distractions over long periods of time) that will affect your calculations. Still, this is a skill worth knowing. Many soldiers from both Vietnam and the Middle East have reported that keeping track of their paces was a key factor in their general navigation.

6

The Compass

— ✕ —

Orienteering with
Magnetic North

"He that has patience may compass anything."

François Rabelais

In its simplest form, the compass is nothing more than a free-spinning, magnetized sliver of metal. Your compass should be a simple workhorse—it doesn't matter if it impresses your friends or not. However, some modern compasses are so simplistic that they are not worth your money. For example, the little compasses that attach to zipper pulls are clever, but are not as durable or sometimes don't have a mechanism that accounts for declination.

Some compasses are very complicated, and cost much more than you need to spend for something reliable. For navigational purposes, obtain an orienteering compass, also known as a baseplate-style compass.

THE PARTS OF A COMPASS

The four primary components that make up an orienteering compass are listed below:

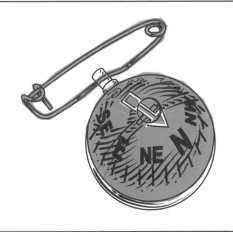

Some outdoor companies sell mini compasses that affix to jackets and zippers. They are more for fashion than wayfinding, and can lack durability and accuracy.

- The baseplate: The clear, rectangular plastic base of the compass upon which the direction of travel arrow is printed. The baseplate is clear so you can see a map through it.
- The direction of travel arrow: The printed arrow on the baseplate, which you point in the direction you intend to travel.
- The dial (also called the "house"): The round dial that turns. It is printed with the orienting arrow and, at the outer edge, ticks in 360 degree increments.
- The needle (also called the "dog"): The magnetic needle that always points to magnetic north.

There may be other features on the compass you own, such as a mirror or sighting line. Read whatever instructions come with your compass to understand all of its features.

MAGNETIC NORTH VERSUS TRUE NORTH

Before using a compass, it is important to understand the difference between magnetic north and true north. True north is at the North Pole, but your compass needle doesn't usually point there. Instead, compasses point to a magnetic zone that is roughly northwest of Hudson Bay in northern Canada. While the reasons for this are debated, most geologists believe that the movement of molten iron in the earth's core acts like a giant generator, creating magnetic north. This magnetic zone is not fixed—it changes about a tenth of a degree every year—but this deviation is so slight that we can use magnetic north as a more or less fixed point for navigation.

WHAT IS DECLINATION?

The angle at which magnetic north deviates from true north is called declination. Declination must be adjusted for when pairing a compass (pointing toward magnetic north) with a map (using true north). Sometimes maps have a little diagram showing how declination should be used to correctly orient with a compass, sometimes it is simply written.

What are the possible ramifications if you don't adjust for declination? Well, part of the answer depends on where you are, as different geographic locations vary in how far off they are. If you were hiking around Seattle, you'd need to account for about 15 degrees, which is fairly substantial, while an excursion around Nashville would mean accounting for only three degrees difference between magnetic and true north. If you are using your compass to guide you over long distances, especially if the declination is significant, NOT accounting for the difference could put you off by miles. In the above example, using an unadjusted compass to travel linearly one mile in the Seattle area would veer you off course by about a quarter of a mile. Depending on your destination, that could prove significant. If your map doesn't give you the necessary information, determining the declination of your area is simple. The National Oceanic and Atmospheric Administration (NOAA) has a simple online tool where you can plug in an address, city, or even zip code. If you are using the declination information printed on your map, ensure that your map was published recently, ideally within the last two years.

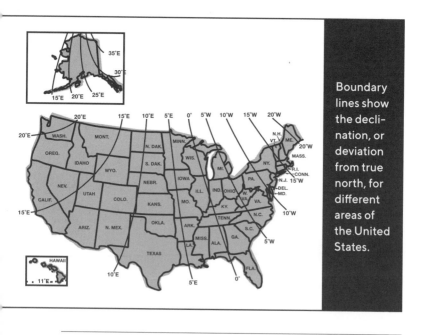

Boundary lines show the declination, or deviation from true north, for different areas of the United States.

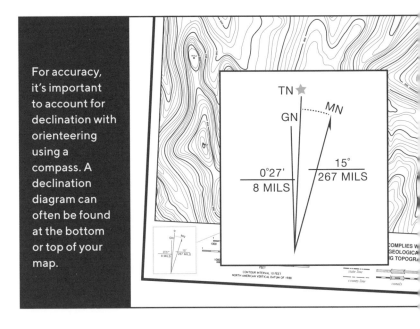

For accuracy, it's important to account for declination with orienteering using a compass. A declination diagram can often be found at the bottom or top of your map.

WEST IS BEST, EAST IS LEAST

The Boy Scout saying goes, "west is best, and east is least," a simple reminder for how to adjust the compass for declination. If you're on the West Coast, turn the dial clockwise, to the right. When on the East Coast, turn the dial counterclockwise, to the left. If you can't remember this technique, simply lay the compass on the map, so that the needle is parallel to the magnetic north line on the declination code. How much you turn the dial depends on where you are in relation to magnetic north, usually marked on the map. The boundary line, zero degrees between true north and magnetic north, runs from Canada south through western Wisconsin down through Florida's panhandle, and beyond. Along that line, there is a negligible difference between true north and magnetic north.

On a typical baseplate compass, each of the little vertical black lines, called tick lines, represent two degrees. So, if you live in Los Angeles and your map indicates an easterly declination of 12 degrees, you would turn the dial clockwise six tick lines.

❝ The Boy Scout saying goes, 'west is best, and east is least.' If you're on the West Coast, turn the dial clockwise, to the right. When on the East Coast, turn the dial counterclockwise, to the left. **❞**

USING A COMPASS

PUTTING THE DOG IN THE HOUSE

Now that you have a basic understanding of the compass, let's use it to get somewhere. In this case, we'll assume that you want to go about four miles, just a bit west of south. There are no obstacles along your way through a forest, so you're able to walk in more or less a straight line. There are a few hills on the path, and at least two dips. You can actually see a distant lookout tower on the hill where you're heading.

Lay compass in the palm of your hand, removing any metal objects which may inhibit the accuracy of the compass, such as keys,

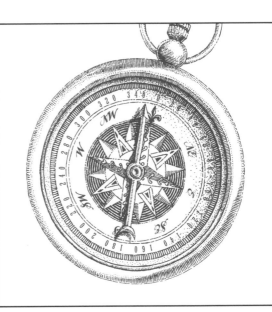

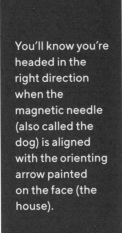

You'll know you're headed in the right direction when the magnetic needle (also called the dog) is aligned with the orienting arrow painted on the face (the house).

watches, or eyeglasses. Point your direction of travel arrow directly at the lookout tower. Next, rotate the dial of your compass so that the orienting arrow (the house) is directly under the magnetized needle (the dog). The point of the 360 degree dial that now lines up with the direction of travel arrow indicates that the lookout tower is at 200 degrees, or southwest from your present location.

WALKING IN A LINE AND RETURNING

Now you can start walking toward your destination, the lookout tower. As long as you keep the dog in the house, and follow the direction of travel arrow, you will walk in a straight line ending at the tower. The trip might take longer than you expected, perhaps fog will roll in as you walk, obscuring the lookout tower. Just keep walking at 200 degrees.

Finally, you get to the lookout tower and decide to return to your previous location. Without touching the dial, hold the compass flat and simply turn your entire body so that the opposite end of the needle—typically white or black—is now in the house in place of the dog. Now just follow the direction of travel arrow until you get back to your starting point.

WHY ARE THERE 360 DEGREES IN A CIRCLE?

As far as we know, our current system for dividing time into units of measurement comes to us from the same ancient Mesopotamian culture that gave us the wheel. They were the first to divide time into sixty units—what would become sixty minutes in an hour (and sixty seconds in a minute). The ancient Egyptians then applied this elegant measurement system to circles. They found that a circle can be divided up evenly into six triangular sections. By assigning 360 degrees as the total unit measurement of the circle, each of the triangular sections would then measure 60 degrees. We can also thank the Egyptians for coming up with the circular degree.

CHARTING A COURSE

If you used your compass and a watch to track your travels throughout the days, and recorded those observations in a notebook, it's easy

Having a pen and notebook handy when you're exploring the wilderness allows you to take notes and plot an effective course.

to then chart the most direct way back to your camp or vehicle. This method, which requires a compass, a pen and notebook, and a watch, works in any weather on any terrain, day or night.

The first step is to record the "degree of travel" and how long you walked for each leg of your journey in your notebook. To determine the degree of travel, point the direction of travel arrow on your compass in the direction you are traveling. Next, put the dog in the house by turning the round dial until the orienting arrow is directly over the north end of the needle. The number on your compass that corresponds with the direction of travel arrow is your degree of travel.

Let's give this a try. Say you've driven to a remote area in the forest and you want to explore the surrounding area all afternoon rather than following an established trail. Draw two columns in your notebook, one for degrees and one for time. You set out at 260 degrees and walk until you hit a natural stopping point, say for ten minutes. Stop, and record 260 in the degrees column and 10 in the time column. Now you change directions, heading out at 140 degrees. This time, you walk for thirty minutes before you pause, so you record 140 in the degrees column and 30 in the minutes column.

You continue this way for the rest of the day, always recording the degree in which you walked, and the amount of time you walked in that direction. If one leg of your journey was uphill and you had to walk more slowly, you make a note of that. If you had to slow down to cross a stream, you make a note of that as well. And if you covered terrain more rapidly on a downhill section, you make a note of that as well (see pacing, pages 90–93). For this system to work optimally, you need to walk in a fairly straight line for each leg of your journey. In extremely rugged terrain, this system might not be practical or possible. To determine when you begin a new leg, you can use points of interest to mark a pivot, such as unusual rock formations, or a particularly striking tree.

Now it's time to review, and attempt to create a map from, your notes. Let's say your notebook contains five entries, noting the degree traveled and time traveled. You could use your homemade map to trace your steps back to your starting point. Or, armed with that information, you can find a straight path back to your starting point. Here is an example of what your notes might look like.

TRAVEL DIRECTION	
Degree	Time (minutes)
260	10
140	30
60	40
100	10
330	30

In this example, we have chosen units of time that are divisible by ten. In real life, your units of time would likely be more diverse.

Use your notebook to turn the units of time into linear lengths. For example, ten minutes of time traveled will now be equal to one inch. It doesn't really matter whether you represent each ten-minute leg as one inch or five inches or the length of your finger—so long as you are consistent with whatever unit of conversion you use.

In this example, we're going to use sticks to create a map. To represent the first ten-minute leg of your journey, cut a straight stick so that it is one inch long. Lay the stick on the ground and align it at 260 degrees, your direction of travel. The next leg of your journey was thirty minutes, so cut a stick that is three inches long. From the leading end of the first stick, set down your three-inch-long stick and align it at 140 degrees. Continue to add sticks representing length at the degrees traveled until you have created a map of your journey.

When you have completed your map, place your compass at the end of the last stick (which represents where you were when you decided to go home), and point the direction of travel arrow toward your starting point. That is your direct line back to your camp.

It's important to pay attention to how long it takes to walk somewhere when trying to find your way. A simple wristwatch can be used to track the minutes ticking by.

Because you chose one inch to represent ten minutes of travel, you can just measure the distance between your starting point and your ending point to get a good idea of how long it will take you to get back to your camp or car. In this scenario, you would be walking at 248 degrees for about forty minutes. Not bad considering it took you two hours to get to your current location.

While this system works best if your speed is more or less the same, you should also be sure to record any changes in speed as you hike in your notebook, especially on uneven terrain. For example, you would probably cover less terrain in ten minutes on an uphill than you would if the ground were flat. If you walked for twenty minutes, on a steep uphill, you might estimate your time with just a one-inch stick for that leg of the journey.

What if you walk at 248 degrees for the estimated forty minutes and don't end up back at camp? Number one, don't panic. Likely you just had some ups and downs in your day's journey that weren't perfectly represented in the dimensions of your stick map. Perhaps there is some prominent feature that might make your camp recognizable. Can you get to a high point (like up a tree) and see if the camp is visible?

Even up in a tree, you still don't any sign of your camp. The next step is to mark where you are with a pile of stones, or a cord around a tree, or something similar. Hopefully, you won't come back to this point.

Now, begin to make a clockwise circle around this point. Be very observant. Keep circling around and around, making a slightly bigger circle each time. Eventually, you should find your camp.

If you don't like the looseness of continually making a larger circle, try making squares. Walk ten paces north from your ending point, then ten paces east, then twenty paces south, twenty pages west, thirty paces north, thirty paces east, forty paces south, etc., always continually expanding your area. Unless you made some very serious errors while recording the legs of your journey, you will soon find your camp.

GETTING AROUND OBJECTS USING YOUR COMPASS

There are many ways to navigate the landscape using your map and compass. Here's a way to get around obstacles you might encounter,

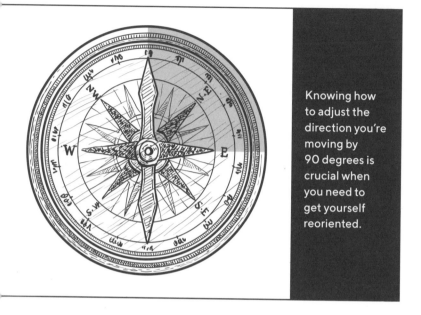

Knowing how to adjust the direction you're moving by 90 degrees is crucial when you need to get yourself reoriented.

using all of the skills you've learned so far. This could be a tree downed by heavy rains or a rock slide on the trail. In this example, we'll keep it simple.

You're traveling east to your destination, which means that you are traveling at 90 degrees (south is 180, west is 270, and north is zero or 360 degrees). You come to a large obstacle in the middle of your path. Your goal is to get around that obstacle and then get back on your route, traveling 90 degrees. You can either go around that obstacle by walking three sides of a square, or by walking two sides of a triangle. While this is very simple geometry, it can get confusing.

THE SQUARE

Start by making a 90-degree right turn. Count your paces until you think you have cleared the obstacle, then make another turn, 90 degrees to your left. Walk until you have cleared the obstacle (it's not necessary to count paces here). Turn 90 degrees to the left again. Walk the same number of paces you travelled on the first leg of your detour. You will now be back in line with your original line of travel. Turn right 90 degrees and continue on your way.

It doesn't matter what direction you were originally traveling when you do this. Just make the right turn, left turn, and left turn, all 90-degree angles, and get back to your original path.

FINDING NORTH WITHOUT A MAGNET

A commonly used non-magnetic compass is the gyrocompass, which has a disc-like component that spins quickly, using the Earth's rotation to find geographical direction automatically.

If you ever find yourself navigating over water, gyrocompasses have significant advantages over magnetic compasses:

- They locate true north based on the axis of the Earth's rotation, which is more useful when navigating than magnetic north.

- They are unaffected by ferromagnetic materials, like a ship's steel hull, which can distort the magnetic field.

OTHER KINDS OF COMPASSES

THE THUMB COMPASS

Introduced by Suunto in 1983, the Norcompass was the first commonly used "thumb compass." Smaller than the traditional variety, a thumb compass is commonly used in orienteering activities, where map reading and understanding the terrain is critical. Unlike the standard magnetic compass, thumb compasses have very little markings on them, oftentimes having no degree numbers showing at all. They are typically used only for the purpose of orienting a map to magnetic north.

The thumb compass can be conveniently attached to the user's thumb by securing it with a small elastic band. By using an oversized needle to point north, these compasses allow those who are familiar with the cardinal directions to easily orient themselves based on where the arrow points. Many styles of thumb compasses are transparent, which allows the user to hold a map with the compass laid on top of it, thereby presenting the map through the lens of the compass itself. The most helpful models use rare-earth magnets which provide the most accuracy, reducing needle settling time to one second or less.

Thumb compasses can be used for hiking, mountaineering, and even adventure racing. Once you get used to the small size and versatility of the thumb compass, you may find yourself rarely using a larger compass anymore.

THE EQUILATERAL TRIANGLE

This time there is a large object preventing you from proceeding left or right from your position, but it is possible to move around the object blocking the path directly in front of you by cutting diagonally. In this instance, it makes sense to use the triangle detour. Use the same method as above, but this time you walk on two sides of a triangle at 60 degrees, rather than three sides of a square at 90 degrees.

7

Beyond a Map and Compass

—— ✕ ——

Techniques for GPS
and Smartphones

"Maps codify the miracle of existence."

Nicholas Crane

Knowing how to use a map and compass to find your way through unknown territory is a skill that will never go out of style. It could even save your life someday. But it's not possible to have a map for every single place you might find yourself. Most people only buy maps for the areas they live in and travel to regularly.

Fortunately, there are now a number of apps on smartphones and various GPS devices that almost render the map and compass obsolete . . . almost. A map should always be carried as backup should your technology fail you. GPS devices or smartphones can sometimes be slow to find a satellite connection in a wooded area or in places where the sky is obscured by tall objects. They can also run out of battery, or be accidentally broken, dropped in a river, or left out in the rain.

There are also a number of things that are easier and quicker to do with a map and compass:

- Find the shortest route to a particular point.
- Find the easiest route to a particular point.
- Find the easiest way around a mountain.

- Chart a course to an unseen destination.
- Chart a course that passes through differing environments.
- Find the best route that allows you to stay on the highest terrain.
- Choose a hiking route that allows you to avoid as much contact with civilization as possible.
- Go directly to a campsite.
- Go directly to water sources.
- Go directly to a specific structure.
- Chart a safe cross-country, off-trail course.
- Create challenging games with youth groups.

But GPS technology is also advancing all the time. Let's take a brief look at how these tools aid in navigation.

PAIRING A GPS OR PHONE WITH A MAP

Navigation applications that can be downloaded on smartphones include Maps.me, MotionX GPS, and BackCountry Navigator. They can be used for offline mapping, tracking routes, and marking waypoints. A GPS unit serves a similar function, but with more geographic accuracy in the backcountry, as GPS devices use satellites to map the exact geographic coordinates of your location, even out of cell range.

Some GPS devices come with a basic map feature, showing the surrounding terrain and its features (such as roads, bodies of water, and trails). Other GPS devices come with maps that are more barebones, and only show tracked dots (or waypoints) along your path.

A GPS SUCCESS STORY

During a canoe trip in a remote part of Minnesota's Boundary Waters, a friend and I set off one morning from the island where we had been camping. The Boundary Waters is a confusing series of interconnected lakes that span thousands of miles, so we packed a GPS unit to help us avoid getting lost. As we paddled along the shore of the lake, we fell deep into conversation. After an hour or so, we looked around and wondered if we had missed the passage to the next lake. We noticed that a nearby island looked familiar, and as we paddled closer, we realized it was the island where we had camped the previous night—back where we started. We had paddled in a large circle. Luckily, we had been marking waypoints on our GPS the whole time, so we were able to compare our course to our map and backtrack to find the passage to our next destination.

To use a GPS device and a map together, first look at the map of the area you'll be traveling through. Locate where you're standing and mark a waypoint of that physical location on your GPS device. Label it something like "trailhead" or "starting point." At the next significant landmark, log another waypoint on your GPS unit. Look back at the map and note the location of the landmark as a frame of reference. Continue this process for the duration of your trip.

8

Exercises

—— ✕ ——

Fun Ways to Build Your Skills

*"In every walk with nature one
receives far more than he seeks."*

John Muir

Just as you wouldn't set up your tent for the first time in the woods, don't wait to practice different methods of navigation until you're in the wild. Here are a few orienteering exercises to help you hone your skills and build confidence before you set out.

EXERCISE 1: THREE-LEG COMPASS WALK

For this exercise, you'll need a compass and a stick or pencil to use as a location marker. Make sure you have enough space to roam around. Place the location marker on the ground, set your bearing due north, or zero degrees, and note a prominent landmark that falls in line with this bearing. Walk fifty paces in the direction of the landmark, and then, from this second location, set your compass bearing for 120 degrees. Find a second landmark that lines up with your new 120 degrees bearing, and walk fifty paces toward it. Next, set your third bearing for 240 degrees, line it up with a landmark, and walk another fifty paces toward this final landmark.

If you set your compass bearings accurately, you should return to the approximate location of your original marker.

EXERCISE 2: CLOSED COURSE

This exercise is best completed with a partner who want to practice their navigation skills. First, draft a list of bearings and paces for each participant. Participants can also take turns writing their own sets of instructions. Your list should look something like this:

- Walk twenty paces east
- Walk thirty paces south
- Walk fifteen paces east
- Walk forty paces north

And so on. You can make the list as long as you like, but the main objective is to have each participant end up at the same place when they are finished. Each participant should carry a compass and a stick or pencil to mark their starting locations. Add a little fun to the game by setting a timer to see who can complete a certain list the fastest. It's a good idea to test your own list first, so that you're sure the participants will return to their starting places when they get to the end of your instructions.

EXERCISE 3: GEOCACHING

Geocaching involves using GPS latitude and longitude coordinates to locate a hidden cache. With GPS capability built into most smartphones, it's an easily accessible way to practice your GPS coordinate skills. A geocache is usually stored in a waterproof box and contains a variety of interesting finds. Fun for all ages, it's like a modern-day treasure hunt!

Given the growing popularity of this activity, geocaches can now be found all over the world—in cities and in nature. Applications like Geocaching can be used to approximate the location of the geocache with GPS coordinates, but then it is up to you to figure out the hiding place from there. Sometimes it's necessary to look at a map to determine the best—and safest—possible route, because natural obstacles, such as rivers, lakes, or cliffs, can stand in the way.

Some geocaches are located in hollowed-out logs, while others are buried under rocks. In cities, geocaches can be found at the base

OTHER BEST GEOCACHE BEST PRACTICES

- Before you set off on a geocache adventure, tell someone where you're going.
- Plot waypoints for your starting location, so that you can find your way back.
- Be sensitive to the natural world. Don't uproot plants or disturb rocks or soil when looking for a geocache. Stay on maintained paths when possible—most geocaches are located just off a trail.
- Look up. When searching for a geocache, there is a tendency to look down at a GPS device, phone, or map while walking. Look up enough to make sure you don't run into dangerous obstacles like poison oak, cliffs, or holes.
- When you find a geocache, sign the log book.
- Some geocaches contain trinkets that you can keep for yourself. If you want to keep a trinket, it's encouraged to leave something in the geocache behind that is of equal or greater value for the next person who finds it. Other items in geocaches are called "travel bugs," designated to be moved from geocache to geocache. They usually come with a tag so you can track where you found it. If you take a travel bug, be sure to place it inside the next geocache you visit.

- When you return home, log your geocache experience online, such as on a smartphone application. This will notify the owner of the geocache that it was found. You can post photos and other information—such as potential hazards that may have developed—as necessary.

If you decide you love geocaching, and want to start hiding some of your own, be sure to follow a few basic best practices:

- Hide your geocache without disturbing the natural world—uprooting or trampling vegetation, digging holes, breaking tree branches, etc. Get creative with where you hide it to minimize the impact to the environment.
- Don't hide the geocache on private property or in national parks, protected wilderness areas, or in a place where these areas must be crossed in order to reach it.
- Don't stash items in the geocache that are offensive, or that will mold, spill, or cause a mess inside the canister.
- Add the geocache to the geocache database on www.geocaching.com or the geocache application of your choosing.

of street lamps, under park benches, and in nooks and crannies in the exteriors of buildings. Some are hidden in plain sight, such as a plastic rock with a geocache inside of it. Geocaching challenges you to elevate your observations (an important tool in navigation!), because the people who hide geocaches come up with clever ways to conceal their locations. Don't forget to look up!

Inside the geocache, you'll find a variety of items. Most geocaches include a log book, where you can write your name and the date you located the cache. Some geocaches also include trinkets like plastic toys, currency from around the world, inexpensive jewelry, and useful items like stress relief balls or insect repellent wipes.

One of the tricky parts of geocaching is that sometimes the people hiding the geocaches lack an accurate GPS device or precise navigation skills. This can mean that you could find the physical location of the geocache's coordinates, but still be ten to twenty feet from the actual geocache site, due to human or technological error.

Final Advice

As you can see when you dive into the art and science of navigation, there is more to understand than just traveling from point A to point B. Humans have been honing our navigation skills and technology for centuries. But as sophisticated as our navigation technology has become, aspiring navigators should learn the basics first. A compass and a map are your two most reliable tools for finding your way, and should always be carried as backup in case your tech devices fail you.

❝Unpredictable natural conditions—weather, currents, natural obstacles—can challenge even the most seasoned outdoorsperson.❞

It's also important to remember that unpredictable natural conditions—weather, currents, natural obstacles—can challenge even the most seasoned outdoorsperson. Most people who spend time in the outdoors have a "the time I got lost" story. Usually, these stories begin with, "I left my compass and map behind." That's why it is so crucial to pack the essentials, practice your skills before you have to employ them in a dangerous situation, and know how to stay calm and use your knowledge to find your way to safety.

Expanding your knowledge of navigation can open doors to new hobbies like stargazing, survivalism, and fashioning sundials. Teach friends your new skills and volunteer to be the map keeper on road trips and hikes. Study maps just for the fun of it and learn about areas of interest in your region. Observe how the constellations move through the night sky and note how they change over the course of the year. Research how ancient civilizations developed their own navigational systems, and marvel at how the early explorers mapped the entire globe over hundreds of years of dangerous voyages. Perhaps after reading this book, you'll feel inspired to do some exploration of your own.